THE SPARTAN CHRONICLES

The Spartan Chronicles

THOMAS FROOD

Somewhat Grumpy Press Inc

Edited by DA Brown.

This work is a memoir based on personal recollections and historical events. It reflects the author's present recollections of experiences over time. Some names and characteristics have been changed, some events have been compressed, and some dialogue has been recreated. The author and publisher in no way represent any company, corporation, or brand, mentioned herein. The views expressed in this memoir are solely those of the author.

Published by arrangement with Somewhat Grumpy Press Inc.
Halifax, Nova Scotia, Canada. www.SomewhatGrumpyPress.com
The Somewhat Grumpy Press name and Pallas' cat logo are registered trademarks.

ISBN 978-1-7387998-4-8 (paperback)

ISBN 978-1-7387998-5-5 (eBook)

First Printing - October 2023 v2

Contents

Chapter 1

Introduction

The Spartan Chronicles is a collection of stories about places, people, and events which occurred years ago while I was working for Spartan Air Services in the Canadian North as a radio operator and weather observer.

Chapter 2

Reminiscing

One of life's treasures is reminiscing with old friends. In general, your buddies will want to hear what you have to say provided they are given ample opportunity to recollect back at you. Possibly the purpose in telling stories is to revisit the past for a while, to reconsider what has been seen or done, and regain the feeling of having experienced something worthwhile. One would hope that life and living would contain memories worthy of being talked about later. Often the humour evoked by these reflections is priceless. Laughing out loud with your friends is good fun and good for you.

Thinking about the significant happenings in our lives may hearken back to olden times when our bygone ancestors were gathered at their campfires, staring into the embers, lost in thought. Some would begin to tell their own stories having been stirred by the rousing anecdotes of others. At times, reflecting on the past may focus on the earlier years, those "back-in-the-day" occurrences, where the bulk of living still lay ahead. Perhaps the significance of these earlier times was not fully appreciated at the time. For some and to a certain extent these earlier undervalued times were wasted but fortunately not forgotten.

Chapter 3

Orientation

The beginning week at Uplands Airport in Ottawa of my first season working for Spartan Air Services was ending with a lot of paperwork. Spartan had hired several of us as radio operators and weather observers, two essential roles in their map-making business. Our orientation centred on the usual paperwork and some testing for special radio operating licences with the Department of Transport as it was called in those days. Reviewing and elevating our weather measuring and observing skills and obtaining the RCMP security clearances filled up the remaining time. This RCMP security clearance requirement seemed to be a bit of a mystery. What did it mean? Likely we were missing some important information. Routine governmental red tape was one explanation. We did not see the bigger picture just yet.

At the time it seemed northern Canada had become some kind of a military arena exemplified by the installation of its many radar facilities spread across mid-Canada and also further north up across its high Arctic regions.

These mid-Canada sites and DEW-line radar monitoring facilities were set up as an early warning system against the threat imposed by the USSR at the time. The United States and its allies including Canada were engaged in a Cold War. The fear of attack by Soviet ICBMs was the underlying main issue. Our recently hired newbie radio and weather group were not fully appreciative of these events taking place throughout Canada's north and the world generally. We were narrowly focused on getting work experience and earning money for next year's tuition.

Our orientation at Uplands Airport was about getting us to understand more fully Spartan's purpose and processes in the topographical map making business. We saw this Human Resource's perspective as important, but our appointed frontier was soon to be doing our job in northwest British Columbia at Fort Nelson, the southern part of the Yukon Territory at Whitehorse, northern Alberta near Fort McMurray, and at Norman Wells in the Northwest Territories. There was also a future job prospect for next season. We could be hired to go further north into the Arctic.

While we were putting in time waiting to fly out to these northern destinations, I guessed Human Resources was at a loss of what to do with us for the remaining two days before our departure. What better way to occupy us than to put our supposed electronics expertise to work in some way to fill-in the time. Our HR handler turned to the technical department of the company, and we were directed to Charlie Norris.

Charlie Norris was some kind of electronics expert in charge of Spartan's magnetometers. The magnetometer devices, installed in Spartan's Anson aircraft, were used in geophysical surveys to find and record the extent of mineral deposits. Spartan Air Services, in addition to its aerial photo surveying for topographical map making, provided magnetometer information for mining companies in Canada as well as for the Columbian Government in South America.

Mining companies and government agencies in both countries were keen to get information about their natural geological deposits. Spartan was able to gather this information for them using its magnetometer services. This was how Spartan made some of its money. The magnetometers were installed and maintained by Spartan's technical department with Charlie Norris in charge.

Charlie did not seem too pleased with his newly foisted responsibility of supervising us if only for a day or so. His disinclination was written all over his face when we showed up for our assignment. In an impatient manner, pointing to an Anson aircraft on the hangar floor, Charlie said, "Get started with that aircraft. Go ahead and strip the Anson."

Charlie may have been a technical expert, but I was soon to discover his weakness was in communicating precise information to lowly inexperienced help like us. He had little understanding of our inexpertise. He had really over-estimated what we knew about magnetometers and airplanes. We had been specifically hired for radio and weather communications related to aerial photography, but we were eager to do anything Spartan asked us to do.

Now to unskilled aircraft workers like us the statement, "*Strip the Anson*," was a vague imperative. One possible interpretation was for us to take the directive literally. To be safe, Bill Dormer, our group's unappointed spokesperson asked, "We are to remove the Anson's electronic gear?" As radio operators we knew something about electronic gear. I guessed Bill had carefully worded this question expecting *"yes"* as the answer, but we waited for some additional follow-up information from Charlie. Follow-up information did not come.

"Yes! Get started now!" Charlie's irritated terse reply was certainly explicit as he turned away to continue working on some other magnetometer conundrum.

In hindsight, we now know what "*Strip the Anson*" means. Installing and maintaining the magnetometers was the focus of Charlie's work, and "*Strip the Anson*" was his code for, "*Remove the magnetometer devices from the aircraft.*" This simple process should have taken at most about half an hour to complete. For us, at that time, we misinterpreted "*Strip the Anson*" to mean, "*Remove all the electronic gear.*" We assumed this task would also include the magnetometer devices as well as a prodigious array of the other electronic devices.

Anson aircraft are replete with electronics, like its array of UHF and VHF transmitters and receivers, as well as the intricate magnetometer recording paraphernalia with each and every device having been installed to DOT (Department of Transportation) specifications. "Well let's get started," said Bill. Bill taking charge of this situation was fine with the rest of us. Our group pitched in to "*Strip the Anson,*" wanting to demonstrate some sort of expertise but mainly to show our willingness to serve the company, to reinforce Spartan's faith in hiring us. We saw ourselves as responsible employees.

We worked diligently with wrenches, wire-cutters, and screwdrivers and soon the pile of gear coming out of the inside of the Anson grew on the hanger floor. The pile of electronic innards represented our diligence and hard work. To extract some of the devices, like, the array of radio transmitters and receivers as well as the magnetometer recording equipment, we had to dismantle some of the supports and interior panelling of the aircraft. It was simple satisfying hard work.

"What the hell?" Charlie's voice boomed throughout the hanger.

Startled, we looked out from inside the aircraft and saw Charlie charging toward the Anson across the hangar floor. He stopped near the pile of parts trying to catch his breath.

"We're stripping the Anson." Bill's statement had a slightly wary and defensive tone to it.

For a moment I thought Charlie was yelling at someone else. Then for an instant I thought he might be having an attack of some kind because of his unusual behaviour and florid appearance. Then my attention focused on the pile of parts on the hanger floor beside the Anson and I knew our dismantling action was the source of his upset.

Charlie had stopped beside the pile gasping for breath searching for words. Explosively, he just muttered, "Get away!" These were the last words I ever heard him utter. I guessed we had really blundered. We now realized we had erroneously eviscerated the Anson. Defensively Bill asserted that it would be a simple matter to reinstall the dismantled gear. Again, Charlie's explosive unintelligible mutterings indicated that we were once again in error.

Later, as we assembled in the Human Resources common room trying to rationalize our ineptitude, we knew our attempts were just lame excuses at regaining some sense of worth. Our mistake surely would cost Spartan considerably. Our HR handler seemed more remote than before perhaps wishing the nightmare to be over as soon as possible. I began to feel our job possibilities may have plummeted from being hired to being fired.

But Spartan did not fire us. I guess they really needed our services elsewhere for other reasons and we were probably the only available candidates at that point. It seems there are not many shortcuts to tempering lack of experience, and the way to gaining some common sense is usually paved with mistakes. The next day as I boarded the commercial Trans-Canada Air Lines turbo-engine Viscount flight out of Ottawa to head west to Edmonton and on to Fort Nelson in northern BC my parting thought was, "I hope Charlie has survived this ordeal." I never saw Charlie again.

Chapter 4

Espionage

In pre-satellite times Spartan Air Services provided geological and topographical information for Canadian and Columbian business corporations and governmental agencies. Because of snow-cover Spartan's topographical aerial surveying in Canada took place during the North American summer months and in and around Bogota, Columbia, South America, during the North American winter months. In this way Spartan could extend its business opportunities with earnings all year round.

For its topographical mapping Spartan used Mosquito aircraft equipped with high-resolution cameras to photograph the terrain from an altitude of thirty-thousand feet where one inch at the on-board camera subtended about nine linear miles of terrain below. The strips of photographic information gathered were then passed on to the relevant government or business agencies to be processed to make topographic maps. Canadian sovereignty was likely the underlying motivation for its aerial photography at that time, particularly the photography of the Arctic

Archipelago. Canada shared a disputed Arctic border with the USSR. The Cold War certainly had heightened many other related issues.

The aerial photo business is very exacting work requiring almost perfect weather conditions including a minimum snow-cover, very little forest fire smoke interference (not a problem in the treeless Arctic but further south it was a definite factor), a certain critical range of sun-angles to reduce shadows (time of daylight), and accurate positioning of the airplanes flying their photo-line sorties. CAVU (Ceiling and Visibility Unlimited) weather conditions were ideal but a rarity. The terrain's photo images gathered by the Mosquitos' cameras were then delivered to and processed by the mapping agencies to form the basic information for topographical maps. Topographical maps are a detailed, accurate graphic representation of the features that appear on the Earth's surface, including both human-made and natural features. The conditions for high quality photographing were exacting and it was rare to have all the right conditions available for more than a few days a season in any one specific location. Everyone, including pilot, navigator, and camera operator had to be ready to do their jobs when it came time to fly photo sorties. In this regard, weather forecasting and communicating was paramount.

In my first season with Spartan, we were attempting to complete the bits and pieces of the unfinished photo-contracts in northern British Columbia and in the south-eastern region of the Yukon Territory. CF HMP, the Mosquito aircraft I was working with, would be flying photo-sorties out of Fort Nelson BC and Whitehorse YT throughout the summer. The DOT airfields at these locations were sufficient to accommodate the Mosquito's maintenance needs and take-off and landing requirements. Next season Spartan would be photo-surveying further north in the Arctic Islands and would be flying out of Cambridge Bay (an Arctic DEW-line site) situated on the southern coast of Victoria Island. The prospect of that job next season was of great interest to me.

But now my specific assignment was to fly TCA from Ottawa to Edmonton and PWA from Edmonton to set up my radio station at Fort Nelson BC. My boss, Mike Grey, was to join me later. The Mosquito airplane CF HMP I would be working with was crewed by pilot Jack Tustin, navigator Bennie Lynch, and camera operator Ken Tustin, Jack's younger brother. At Fort Nelson, as a radio operator and weather observer, I would be responsible for relaying company information to and from Ottawa, processing and communicating weather information from the Department of Transport facilities located at the Fort Nelson and other airfields, and handling some air-traffic control when CF HMP was flying photo-line sorties. I would share weather information throughout the radio network we had set up over north-western Canada with VHF radio stations at Whitehorse YT, Norman Wells and Yellowknife NWT, Fort McMurray Alta, and Fort Nelson BC.

At that time, I could not have imagined the USSR, the US, and the Cold War would enter into the picture. The on-going political enmity between the United States and the Soviet Union and their respective allies apparently was heating up. I did not know that Fort Nelson was a restricted military Air Force base including its role as a mid-Canada Early Warning "listening" site with its monitoring focused on the USSR's radio traffic. Whenever I hear references made about the USSR and the Cold War with the nuclear ICBM threats and deterrents that had polarized the entire world for many years I am reminded of my sojourn at Fort Nelson. In the first place I think I was very lucky not to have been arrested for my inadvertent unauthorized entry onto that military airbase. At the time, I did not realize I was about to enter that high-security military zone and my infringement would go completely unnoticed. A combination of factors led me to be very fortunate in a bizarre kind of way mainly because of my inexperience, my naivety.

Before my departure from head office back in Ottawa I had asked several people for their take on how to go about setting up a radio station at a RCAF airfield. Mike Grey, my very busy and mainly absentee boss, had been rather unclear with his instructions when I did see him. I asked some of my fellow-operators what they were going to do. Of course, each radio station set up would have its own unique requirements.

Fortunately, my inquiries fell on the ears of one Spartan employee, an older ex-serviceman who had been a Flight Sergeant in the old RCAF back in the day. His advice was that I should contact a Flight Sergeant as soon as I got to Fort Nelson and get his advice on how to go about setting up my radio station at the airfield. He said, "Flight Sergeants make things happen on any airbase. In fact, they, for the most part, run the air force." This advice seemed rather simple, and I decided to take it. It was to be my basic game plan, call it "*Operation Flight Sergeant.*"

My late-night mid-May PWA arrival at the airfield at Fort Nelson BC was in the midst of a moderate snowstorm where I found, unexpectedly and much to my chagrin, there were really two Fort Nelsons. One Fort Nelson was the airbase at which I had just landed and practically invisible in darkness and blowing snow. The other Fort Nelson was a small town situated several miles from the airfield on mile two-hundred and sixty of the Alaska Highway. The Alaska Highway is over 1300 miles long and runs from Dawson Creek, BC to Delta Junction, Alaska, and was built during the Second World War.

I was informed by the lone airport attendant that I would have to get a room in town. This was a surprising twist in that there were actually two Fort Nelsons, the airbase and the town. Which location was my real destination? I guessed it would likely be the airport, but I would deal with that problem in the morning. The taxi driver patiently waited while I loaded my two hundred pounds of radio gear and personal stuff into his cab, and off we drove to the small town of Fort Nelson where I got a room at the only motel.

By next morning the weather had cleared somewhat, and I was eager to get on with "*Operation Flight Sergeant.*" Again, I loaded my gear into the same taxi and headed out to the other Fort Nelson, the airfield, where I had landed the night before. I had decided the airfield was my logical destination, not the town at mile two-sixty. As we neared the airbase I was amazed at the amount of air-traffic. American US fighter jets thundered low and fast over the northern terrain. The roar of their landing and taking off was deafening. The taxi driver indicated the aircraft were USAF F86 all-weather fighters. He said these aircraft were being ferried up the west coast from California to Alaska. "They gas up here at Nelson," he said.

Up to this point my understanding was that Fort Nelson was just a regular Department of Transport RCAF airfield not a full-fledged active military Air Force base. At the gatehouse the sentries waved us through, and, upon reflection, I think they saw me as just another commercial airline passenger on his way out to Grande Prairie or Edmonton. I instructed the taxi-driver to take me to that hanger, and I pointed to the one nearest at hand. This place looked as if it might contain a Flight Sergeant. I unloaded my gear at the side-entrance and stood there amidst my radio equipment and my personal belongings with the roar of jets all around me. Inside I asked an airman where I might find the Flight Sergeant. "Flight Sergeant Grant is in his office over there." He pointed across the hangar.

Flight Sergeant Grant seemed somewhat puzzled at first. "Spartan Air Services? Oh yes, those speedy Mossies. Now I remember. They were flying out of Whitehorse last summer. So, you need to get set up here, eh? Well, I think we can handle that."

My needs were very efficiently met by Flight Sergeant Grant. I saw that Flight Sergeants probably did run the airbase. He showed me accommodations in the officer's quarters, a comfortable room, with my radio equipment to be conveniently located in an adjoining space. The nearby Officer's Mess had a lounge and bar with plush chairs, darts, and a pool table. He also showed me the cafeteria in another nearby building where I would get my meals. Lodging, food, recreation, and purpose seemed to come together in a rush. I was in business. "*Operation Flight Sergeant*" was an outstanding success.

Soon I got the VHF and UHF radio equipment set up and operating. For my VHF transmitter and receiver, I strung a straight 40-metre wire antenna from the peak of the officer's quarters' building to one of the poles in the backstop of the softball diamond. Upon testing the gear everything worked perfectly. Over the next few days, I made contact with the other stations on our radio network and in conversation described my setup. Their reactions indicated that things in Norman Wells and Fort McMurray were far from perfect. They were not situated on military airbases like me but at civilian Department of Transport airfields where they likely had to endure their own cooking.

When it came to meals the cafeteria fare at Fort Nelson was superb. Eggs, bacon, steak, roasts, potatoes, vegetables, homemade bread, and pie were standard offerings prepared by real cooks. I wondered how much these accommodations were going to cost. Flight Sergeant Grant had not mentioned anything about costs. Perhaps he would send me a statement when the time came for billing. In any event I expected Spartan would cover the expense.

Over the next two weeks I managed to fit into the hustle and bustle at the airbase quite well. I was referred to as, "Tom! He's with Spartan's Mossies. Radio and weather." The air force service people were very friendly and helpful. During mealtime, I met an LAC whose job was to monitor radio traffic emanating from the USSR. He was a radio operator using state of the art communication devices. What an interesting job I thought. We became friends and he gave me a tour of the mid-Canada monitoring-site and showed me what he did. His work-area consisted of banks of recording devices, like delicate radio receivers, tape recorders, and beam-antennas.

I received information via our radio network indicating CF HMP was undergoing some final maintenance in Edmonton and would arrive as soon as the weather conditions for photo became likely. I was also informed that my boss Mike Grey would be flying out from Ottawa to meet with me in about a week to get me set up on the Fort Nelson airbase. What a strange message I thought. I was set up and operating on a daily basis. I would surprise him.

Mike Grey finally arrived, and I met him at the airplane. The first thing he said was he had been in contact with Canadian Government military officials, the Department of Transport, and the RCMP. He said he had also communicated with the base commanding officer here at Fort Nelson. We were to meet with him the next day about getting me set up on the airbase. At that point I interrupted him and proclaimed that I was already set up on the base and operating. I then briefly told him about "*Operation Flight Sergeant*" and that I had been making network transmissions several times a day for a few weeks.

He nearly fell over in disbelief. "You've done what? That's not possible. This airbase is a mid-Canada monitoring facility. No one is allowed to operate on this base without authorization and I am arranging it right now." Quickly his disbelief became concern and then his worry seemed to change to consternation.

It was only then I realized the situation. How stupid of me. What embarrassment and repercussions would my unofficial infiltration onto this military airbase cause? My unknowing and unknown intrusion surely must have violated some sort of security protocol. Besides Mike Grey, it seemed no one else was aware of my unauthorized presence on the airbase. Somehow, I had unintentionally and unwittingly bypassed military security. I now realized I had entered onto this high-security airbase without official permission. Was this action criminal?

Thoughts, like the Cold War, the USSR, heightened security, and espionage suddenly rushed at me. How would my intrusion affect my employer, Spartan Air Services? Would Spartan now be prohibited from using the airfield? Would this breech result in Spartan losing a photo contract? What would happen to Flight Sergeant Grant who had assisted me in getting set up? Would that tour of the mid-Canada radio listening facility get my LAC friend in trouble? These questions churned through our conversation as my boss and I talked things over. We decided to form some sort of a rescue plan to try to mitigate the situation. We knew our rescue plan would not be perfect, but we could think of no other way.

Very quietly and as unobtrusively as possible, like thieves in the night, we dismantled the radio equipment in the officer's quarters and loaded it into that same taxi as before and headed for town and its motel once again. The taxi-driver never said a word, but he must have wondered what was happening. We would return to the airbase tomorrow and officially present ourselves and follow-up on Spartan's request for accommodations and a place to set up my radio station. On our way out past the gatehouse I looked back and noticed the VHF transmitter's 40-metre wire antenna strung between the officers' quarters and the ball diamond's backstop. It was incriminating evidence.

The next day our meeting with the base commanding officer was very tense as we were welcomed onto the airbase. I was worried the commanding officer might recognize me because I had seen him several times previously in the cafeteria at mealtime and at the ball diamond during ball games. He assured me that I would receive any help I needed, and that I would find the officers' quarters and the cafeteria more than adequate. He indicated that Spartan would be billed directly for all costs. With mixed emotions but mainly relief we thanked him for his help. The absurdity of the situation was almost overwhelming as I hoped my intrusive actions would not be discovered. As far as I know they never were, and I look back at those events and wonder how I ever managed.

Our aerial photo sorties began a little later when photo conditions were right. We were successful in completing most of the bits and pieces of unfinished photo contracts in northern BC. Later that summer our team moved to Whitehorse, and we completed some of the photo contracts in the south-eastern region of the Yukon. We all worked hard not missing any opportunities over the remainder of the summer.

That first season with Spartan ended tragically in mid-September with the crash of our Mosquito CF HMP near Neepawa, Manitoba killing the pilot and the camera operator, Jack and Ken Tustin. The crash occurred while the aircraft was being ferried to Ottawa to prepare it for the winter's photo contracts in Columbia. Fortunately, navigator Bennie Lynch's life was spared. He had taken on the task of driving the car back to Ottawa from Edmonton and had fortunately escaped the fatal crash.

It was with a heavy heart I returned to Queen's that fall burdened with the thoughts of such a terrible loss. No words could possibly describe my feelings about this tragedy. Our CF HMP team of amazing people had worked well together. In any event the job with Spartan had paid well and I was able to cover my tuition fees and some other expenses. Now it was time to settle in and hit the books again. However, already I had thoughts about next season with Spartan in the high Arctic.

Chapter 5

Insertion

It was early-May, and I was anticipating my second season with Spartan. Several of us from the previous year had been rehired to set up temporary weather stations on Victoria Island and Prince of Wales Island in the Arctic Archipelago. Our assignment, myself and fellow operator Gene Marley, was to set up and operate a temporary weather station at Hadley Bay on the north coast of Victoria Island.

Victoria Island is a large Arctic Island lying north of the Canadian continental mainland. It is the eighth largest island in the world and is Canada's second largest island, Newfoundland being the fourth largest. Our weather station was to be located somewhere near the southern end of Hadley Bay at a river's estuary. Hadley Bay runs roughly south to north located slightly west of the north magnetic pole and opening onto the Arctic Ocean and the famous Northwest Passage just south of Melville Island. The weather station was to be located at about 71^0 N latitude 107^0 W longitude. The exact positioning was to be determined by finding a good location on sight.

Once again, I travelled to Ottawa's Uplands Airport to briefly touch base with head office, and then west and north via Edmonton, Yellowknife, and then on to Cambridge Bay where Spartan had its main base for the high-altitude photo gathering Mosquitos. The Otter and Beaver service aircraft used for transporting the equipment to the future weather stations were also stationed at Cambridge Bay.

I imagined the second season would be much different from my first season in northern BC and southern Yukon. Fort Nelson and Whitehorse had been places filled with remarkable people doing interesting jobs. I wondered what a remote Victoria Island and Hadley Bay would have to offer.

Cambridge Bay is on the south coast of Victoria Island across the Dease Strait from mainland Canada on the Arctic Ocean and was our central base from which we would fly to set up our temporary weather stations. The weather station at Hadley Bay was to be situated about two-hundred nautical miles north of Cambridge Bay, Cambridge Bay being a Distant Early Warning or DEW-line site having a good gravel runway for our Beaver and Otter service aircraft, and for the Mosquitos aircraft. Cambridge Bay was sufficiently equipped for the operations of the high-altitude photo-gathering Mosquitos.

Two weather teams each consisting of two persons each were to be flown into their respective locations from Cambridge Bay to the proposed sites at Hadley Bay and Fisher Lake on Prince of Wales Island further to the east of Victoria Island. Our purpose was to observe weather and report this information which would eventually wend its way to the Arctic Forecast Team in Edmonton. These two temporary weather stations were to provide for more precise weather coverage because of the relatively sparse number of regular Department of Transport weather reporting stations spread across the high Arctic. A more comprehensive weather reporting system, including Hadley Bay's and Fisher Lake's weather, was needed to provide the AFT and, eventually, Spartan's aircrews with the information needed to more efficiently complete the remaining photo contracts.

In setting up our weather station our task was to transport our station's tents and stoves, power generator, radio, and weather equipment to a site at Hadley Bay by single-engine Otter equipped with skis for landing on the sea-ice. We were to set up these stations as soon as possible. Gene Marley, my fellow operator, and I flew from Yellowknife to Cambridge Bay where we began preparing the equipment for the final leg of the insertion to Hadley Bay. Marley was about ten years older than me in his final year Meteorology at McGill. I was about to enter my second year of math and physics at Queen's. I knew I was dreadfully inexperienced in the ways of the Arctic, but I thought the biggest challenge would be enduring the many days of isolation we had before us. Over the next three months or so we would be on our own at the remote Hadley Bay location about two-hundred miles from the nearest person. I imagined this venture would be somewhat similar to a space voyage on a trip to the planet Mars, our planet being our weather station at Hadley situated in an outer space universe of the vast high Arctic.

At Cambridge Bay we assembled the equipment into Otter-sized loads under the direction of project manager and pilot Ken Bolam, and from Cambridge we were to make several flights to Hadley to transport our equipment and setup the weather station. The existing but imprecise maps of the area showed a small peninsula near the mouth of an unnamed river flowing northward into the southern end of Hadley Bay. That tiny peninsula was likely to be our weather station's location. Ken had decided this site would be a good place to set up our weather station because at the mouth of the river the flowing water from the interior of the Island should provide adequate landing and take-off possibilities for the Beaver on floats in September. This estuary should be relatively free of ice when it came time for withdrawal. Over the next few weeks, we flew several trips in the Otter to the small jut of land to deliver the equipment, set up the camp, and to get things working. At this mid-May time of the year the Hadley Bay area was covered with snow and ice. The winter still held on.

Our camp consisted of two eight by eight canvas tents each with a small aluminium door wired to an aluminium-pole framed super-structure. We situated the two tents about a hundred feet apart for safety, each tent being heated by a tiny oil stove. Our yellow-painted gasoline Onan generator supplying electric power for the radios was situated midway between the two tents. The radio transmitters, receivers, antennas, weather equipment, food supplies, and personal stuff made up the remaining gear. One tent was for sleeping and the other for cooking and radio communications for weather reporting.

Our VHF radio transceiver was used to report our weather data to Cambridge and to receive communications from the radio network. The UHF radio kept us in contact with the service Otter or Beaver aircraft but mainly with the Mosquitos when they would be flying the high-altitude photo-line sorties. Some air-traffic control for safety was needed and performed by our weather station. We set up and tested all the equipment and everything worked fine. After the last load the Otter took off and droned southward leaving us alone with the winds and blowing snow.

Earlier in April when I was interviewed, the hiring team had asked me a few questions about my experience with winter camping. My response had been that there should be no problem. They took me at my word. Previously I had done some orienteering and had canoe-tripped in the summers in Algonquin, Killarney, and La Verendrye Parks where I had paddled, portaged, and camped, usually a week or so at a time. Surely, I could transfer some of this knowledge to the Arctic venue. My co-worker, Gene Marley, was originally from Ireland. He had spent a year as a weather officer aboard a merchant marine ship. He was a little older and I felt I could rely on his experience. At this early point I could not have imagined what the Arctic had to offer in the way of its subtle challenges.

In the first two weeks we were routinely delivering the weather information for the AFT in Edmonton via Cambridge Bay. At this early stage we sent weather reports to Cambridge every six hours on the hour to test the system's efficacy. Flying photo-sorties at this early stage was not possible because of the snow coverage. We would make the weather measurements and observations and Cambridge would relay our reports to the AFT in Edmonton.

However, at this time of the century our regular VHF radio communications with Cambridge Bay were being disrupted by abnormally energetic solar-flares which caused the ionized layer in the Earth's atmosphere in our polar-regions to alter its normal radio frequency reflective properties. These disruptions, called "white-outs", made our VHF communications uncertain. At times there were no VHF signals whatsoever and sometimes our radio communications were not functional for several days at a time. Our other communication frequencies provided by UHF were for line-of-sight communications with the aircraft and inadequate for contacting Cambridge Bay because of the Earth's curvature.

At this time of year in early June we had continuous variable daylight but the light intensity we were experiencing was greatly reduced by the dense cloud layers covering this coastal region. This filtering of light through the cloud-mass resulted in an eerie grey-white effect that made it very difficult to determine the distance of certain land-features or even estimate the time of day accurately. The grey sky seemed the same colour as the featureless grey-white snow-covered landscape. The sky and the terrain blended together in a strange way.

Even by early June the piercing icy winds that swept across the frozen land still blew the snow into shallow drifts around the yellow-painted Onan generator and our two tents. Our two canvas shelters perched on the small rocky peninsula shook in the wind and the aluminium-pole frames creaked with each gust. When the weather was like this Marley and I were essentially confined to the immediate area of the camp and mainly the tents. We began to wonder how long this dreary tedium would last. Surely the weather would soon change, and we would get a chance to view the terrain now obscured with low cloud cover and blowing snow.

Chapter 6

The Hill

The dreariness of our confinement was broken about two weeks after our arrival at Hadley Bay when the cloud layers lifted somewhat making the visibility much better. The winds had also diminished. With the improved conditions we noticed the faint outline of a low hill in the distance north of our weather station. "How far away is it?" we wondered. The faint outline of the distant hill was intriguing mainly because it was the only discernible feature in our grey-white landscape. The sketchy maps we had used in selecting the location for our weather station were just rough outlines and not topographical at all.

We reacted enthusiastically to the improved weather situation and the sighting of the interesting low hill. We were challenged to get outside and explore to the hill in the distance, to make a trek to investigate. Our vague plan was to make the next weather report on the hour then hike to and investigate the distant hill but return as soon as possible. We could go out and back in about three hours at most. We saw no real problem. The walk would do us good.

We started out by crossing the stretch of heaved sea-ice just north of our campsite. We mounted and descended these icy ridges and made it to the east shore of the Bay and then steadily moved toward the low hill barely discernible in the distance. We welcomed the exercise, but it still required some moderate effort. We trudged along in our parkas, wind pants, and snow boots with a light wind from the south at our backs. The terrain was relatively flat and at no time appeared to slope upward very much toward the distant hill.

After about an hour we stopped. The wind was picking up. To this point the focus had been on getting close to the hill for a better look. Only a little while ago we had turned and looked back toward our campsite in the distance to the south. The tents appeared as two tiny almost invisible specks on a grey-white background. As well, our objective, the low hill to the north, did not appear to be that much closer.

As we continued trudging along, I had a suspicion we may have made a mistake. It can be said that making mistakes teaches you valuable lessons. But sometimes the cost can be high. It began to dawn on me we would not be able to get to the distant hill now and return in the time we had planned. Again, we looked back in the general direction of our campsite. The grey-white canvas specks were no longer visible. Featureless terrain with lightly gusting snow grimily stated this fact. Now we were in trouble. With no tents to view and guide us back to our camp site was a stark realization. I thought we had certainly blundered. But Marley said there should be no problem. "Let's just follow our tracks back until the tents come into view."

Concerned we started back southward into the wind in the general direction of the campsite backtracking on our footprints. At this point I felt a little fatigued. I had heard stories about getting tired, stopping, and resting. Cold and fatigue can do strange things to your judgement. I realized we must get back before too long.

The footprints we were following soon disappeared. The increasing blowing and drifting snow had obliterated them, and we were unsure which direction to take. Somehow, we had gotten off-track, and the visibility was becoming much reduced. I now knew we had a real challenge ahead of us and we had little room for error. From here on we would surely zigzag with no visual references to guide us.

Earlier back at Cambridge I had heard that the Inuit had many words in their vocabulary for the variations in snow and ice conditions. And they knew all about ice and snow. Possibly they needed all these words to differentiate subtle features for their survival. No doubt they had learned about these nuances the hard way.

It occurred to Marley the wind direction was possibly and hopefully our only useful indicator. "The wind has been steady from the south. Let's assume its direction has not changed that much. Let's walk directly into the wind. This line should take us eventually to the shoreline of the bay. Then we can decide which way to go." This tactic was certainly a slim margin to stake our lives on, but we had no other options. So, into the wind we shuffled. I felt weary and now I was getting cold. The wind had increased, and we were bending forward into it with each gust for balance. Visibility had become less than a hundred feet or so and my next thought was that we could pass right by the tents even if we got close and not see them. I hoped we have not yet overshot our campsite.

Suddenly Marley stumbled having bumped into something and fell over in a heap. His voice cracked, “It’s the Onan! We’ve made it!” I peered at the faint outline of the Onan generator its brightly yellow-painted colour just about invisible in the blowing snow. He had accidently stumbled into it, its form fading in and out of view as the blowing snow attempted to drift it over. Soon we were inside our flimsy canvas refuge and safe.

Chapter 7

The Bear

The mid-June weather was moderating. The winds sweeping across the ice of Hadley Bay were still cold, but you could tell the Arctic summer was approaching. The signs of life were all around us especially the cautious seals out on the ice of the bay bobbing at their air-holes. We tried many times to approach them, but it was impossible to get close. I wondered why they were so wary. Surely, in this remote place, they had never encountered any hunters that would do them harm. For that matter, do Arctic seals really think about their safety anyway?

The heaved ridges of sea-ice on the bay were disintegrating in places particularly at the mouth of the river leaving large chunks floating in the estuary as the tides came and went. But the rest of Hadley Bay was mainly iced over. I wondered how extensive the breakup would be. We would need a sufficient expanse of open water at the mouth of the river to accommodate the Beaver on floats for our removal later in early September before next year's freeze-up began.

It had been back in mid-May when we skimmed in the Otter low over the small peninsula to have a look where we would eventually set up our weather station. Surprisingly, we spotted a polar bear running from the sound of our airplane. I thought, "What a magnificent creature." Apparently, it is North-America's largest predator. The bear looked over its shoulder this way and that in an attempt to see what creature could be making all the noise. It did not look up as far as I could tell.

Ken said, "It sure is a fine animal." In retrospect, I think he was just trying to say something positive. Perhaps he thought the sighting of this huge predator would upset us. But it didn't. It didn't upset me because of my naïveté. I did not think once about being down there in the domain of that creature.

Back at Cambridge Bay while preparing the weather station's gear for our insertion I remembered hearing a few stories of polar bears dying at the feet of their hunters having been shot several times in a futile charge. But at that time my thinking was elsewhere. Getting prepared, installing the weather station, and started at our weather and radio assignments was foremost on my mind, call it tunnel thinking.

After unloading the last of the equipment and helping with the final setup Ken had left for Cambridge, the Otter's engine-noise a diminishing sound droning southward. We were on our own. For some reason this fading sound of the Otter's engine noise is still embedded in my awareness. Now we would have to solve our own problems whatever they might be. I never thought again about the polar bear we had seen the first day but, looking back now, it was evident there were some powerful forces at work here.

There were some obvious safety concerns we should have known about.

Shortly before noon I opened the aluminium tent door and stepped outside to start the gasoline-powered Onan generator. To conserve gasoline, we only ran it when we used the radios. The Onan was situated mid-way between our two tents and lately it had been difficult to start. "It's carboned-up. Soon I'll clean the plug." I primed the carburettor and pressed the start-button and it started immediately. Fine and dandy! I turned and stepped back to the radio tent and closed the aluminium door behind me. Out and back in less than half a minute.

Back inside the tent I thought I might have another cup of coffee before the radio schedule. I grabbed my cup, which still had leftover cold coffee grounds in it, turned back to the door, opened it and in one motion tossed the contents outside right into the face of a polar bear not more than an arm's length away. The coffee with some of the grounds dripped down the bear's face which seemed to have an expression of disbelief. The white fur and the dark dripping coffee grounds somehow seemed surreal. The bear was enormous. I slammed the door shut and stood unmoving my pulse pounding with such force it seemed to be coming right out the side of my neck. I was frozen with fear. A huge polar bear just outside. Will it tear its way inside after me? What should I do?

I was very much aware I was inside a flimsy canvas tent. The bear could tear the tent to shreds with one swipe of its enormous claws. I hoped polar bears did not understand canvas. To a polar bear was the tent door the same as the air hole for the bobbing seal? I then suddenly realized the situation out there on the ice of the bay. It was seals versus bears. It was a contest for survival. I saw it was the bobbing air-breathing seals against the stealth of the ever-hungry powerful polar bears. That was the connection I should have made much earlier. That's why the seals were so cautious. I thought about the many times we had walked the ice of the bay totally oblivious to the danger of those invisible bears. They must have been there all along, but we did not see them.

Of course, the canvas tent had no windows. It had no openings to see out of, or to see in for that matter. I listened but no sounds came from outside. Where was the bear? I picked up the camp rifle, a 30-30 Winchester, which was completely unfamiliar to me, thinking it might offer some sort of protection in a desperate situation. It was then I realized the purpose of the camp rifle. I had wondered why we had been issued a rifle with our equipment. Now it was clear. It was for defence. This realization was another association I finally made but hopefully not too late.

My thoughts flashed back to my Model 60 Cooey 22 rifle I had saved up for in my first job at the Simpkin's Egg-Grading Station in Kingston when I was thirteen years old. I had shot at tin cans for target practice at my Uncle Bill's farm but never actually hunted. The stories of the bears I had heard while at Cambridge came flooding back now. In my thoughts were images of a charging polar bear and a skilful hunter firing at it, the bear dying at the feet of its killer just in time. I knew defending by shooting the bear was not for me. As a last resort I would try but my skills and intent did not measure up to the task.

The danger of the situation pounded down on me as I stood there inside the feeble canvas shelter. Survival of the smartest came to mind. I thought about the fact that I had stepped outside and started the Onan, had walked back to the tent, and had not seen or heard the bear. The terrain around the campsite was covered with rocky plate-like shale pieces that clattered when you walked on them. I had not heard any clattering. How close had the bear come to getting me then? I had not heard the bear as it surely had pursued me to the tent after I had started the Onan. This polar bear stealth was remarkable, some kind of predatory behaviour about which I knew absolutely nothing.

I attempted to look out the tiny holes around the doorway where we had wired the aluminium doorframe to the brass grommets in the tent's canvas. I could see nothing through these tiny apertures. I heard no sounds from outside. The bear seemingly was still in its stealth mode. Could It be just around the corner of the tent waiting for me to open the door? I knew the huge predator could be very patient.

To further complicate matters, Marley was asleep in the other tent. Was he in danger? I had to take some kind of action right away just in case. Cautiously, with the rifle ready as it could be, I opened the door a crack, and then a little wider listening and looking in a limited fashion. How much could you really see from a view less than an inch wide? No bear. My heart pounded. I had the door about half-opened when I saw the bear at our garbage dump about a hundred feet away. It was an amazing looking creature, truly magnificent in size and appearance.

With faltering courage, I stepped out and aimed the rifle above and behind the bear deciding to send a shot off into the grey-white Arctic sky hoping the sound of the rifle's report would terrorize it. The hard kick of the rifle was unexpected as the boom and the echo resounded across the estuary. The bear turned toward me but did not run away as I had expected. Oh no, I thought. It just turned and looked at me.

My heart pounded as I sent another round into the air behind it but closer this time. Boom and kick and echo. The bear started to circle. This time, now that it was moving, was the time to act again. I sent the third shot behind it into the rocky shale. Splat! The bear now started to lope away. Thank God, I thought.

Marley came out of the other tent half-asleep and saw the bear as it moved toward the bay. "Did you get a picture?" was all he said.

Marley grabbed his camera and the two of us, me carrying the rifle, took off after the bear as it headed onto the ice amid the huge icy chunks and heaved ridges, and some kind of sanctuary. In less than a minute the bear was gone. It had disappeared. The bear was invisible once again. We had gone some distance after it in our attempt to get our pictures but no bear. No pictures. Disappointed we trudged back to our feeble fragile canvas shelter. I checked the rifle and to my dismay it was out of ammunition. We had been pursuing a polar bear with a loaded camera and an empty rifle.

Chapter 8

The Knock

We had been at Hadley for two months. I felt I was coping fairly well with my isolation at this remote place, but Marley may have been experiencing more unease. I was not sure. The episode with the polar bear had made us extremely cautious. We felt exposed and vulnerable. We knew we were practically defenceless with predators like this prowling around looking for food. Hopefully their usual food, the seals, would suffice. The 30-30 offered no real feeling of security. We knew it was a last resort. We hoped the bears would leave us alone. When we reported the bear intrusion to our main base at Cambridge Bay their response was just short of envy, like, with comments like, "Nothing exciting ever happens around here." They seemed to have classified the polar bear presence as rousing rather than menacing. But what could they do about our situation anyway? When it came to bear intrusions, we were effectively unreachable two-hundred miles away.

Because of the potential danger we did not go far from the tents, always with the 30-30, and ever on the lookout.

Why we felt more secure in and around our fragile canvas tents is still a mystery. Perhaps it was because our insubstantial retreats were all we had and offered our only cover. Regardless, we were constantly on the lookout. Every time I opened the aluminium tent door to go outside the possibility of encountering a polar bear was on my mind.

The bears seemed to be solitary as far as we could tell. We didn't really know how many they were. When we did see one it was always alone. Occasionally we spotted one walking down along the river or out on the ice. Maybe there was only one. It would stand up on its hind legs occasionally to sniff the air or to get a better view. Apparently, their senses of hearing, seeing, and sniffing are excellent. I can't imagine such a magnificent creature having any real deficits. I did not know much about polar bears, but I knew enough to avoid them. After that initial close encounter, we knew one was still in the vicinity and thankfully it seemed to avoid our camp.

About two weeks after the polar bear's intrusion another unnerving event took place. Marley and I were in the radio tent preparing to eat when a knock came from the tent's aluminium door. Then silence. Shaken, my heart pounded something like it had during my polar bear encounter. The polar bear's image flashed through my mind. Were polar bears that polite to knock before entering? Was it just outside waiting? We looked at each other in disbelief but said nothing. The knock on the aluminium tent door had been a definite staccato, "*rap, rap, rap*", and since we had both heard it, it must be real and not just some figment of our imagination brought on by the effect of prolonged isolation. A knock at the tent door under these conditions was most surreal. Marley got up, stepped hesitantly to the door, and cautiously opened it a little bit not knowing what to expect.

Our camp was truly remote. There was no one within two hundred miles as far as we knew, the nearest Inuit settlements being Cambridge Bay to the south and Resolute to the north on Melville Island. Our contact with the outside world was by radio and only when the radio reception made it possible. Apparently, at this time, extreme sun-flare activity was disrupting the ionosphere thereby creating radio “white-outs” for our VHF radio signals. We were even more isolated because of this situation. Not another person for hundreds of miles and sometimes no radio contact with the outside world for several days at a time.

Marley slowly opened the door wider to reveal a person. Standing near the doorway was a bearded man clad in a red chequered bush jacket and baggy wind pants, hiking boots, mitts, and a fur cap. His snow-goggles dangled around his neck. Behind this man, standing in an orderly fashion, were three superb Husky-like dogs each sporting a backpack. For a brief moment the group of six beings stood silently and looked at each other. Marley stepped outside, extended his hand, and wryly said, “We don’t get many visitors here.”

The bearded person introduced himself simply as Brock and indicated he and his dogs were working on a wildlife survey. For his survey he was walking around the coastlines of Victoria Island examining the wildlife in the river estuaries, bays, and lakes and recording his estimate of the varieties and numbers of wildlife. This year marked the third summer he had been doing the survey. He was about fifty years of age and alone except for his three dogs. He seemed in great shape. Brock's dogs were very well-behaved, and they quietly took in this human activity with an occasional wag of their tails. After he had tended to his dogs, Brock shared some tea and conversation with us. He indicated his wildlife survey was sponsored by the University of Alberta.

He said, "I was surveying the estuary and spotted your tents yesterday and decided to pay a visit on my way up the east coast." He revealed he spent about two months every year walking the coasts of several Arctic islands surveying the wildlife populations. He carried no firearm or radio. Apparently, he had an aircraft drop off about a month ago and a pickup prearranged for the end of August at a location somewhere further north along the coast.

We chatted for a while sharing our stories, but soon he was packed up again and, on his way wishing us well. Perhaps he was not used to all the people and wished to regain solitude with his dogs, or he may have just wanted to get on with his task. I was amazed at Brock's ability to manage so well being alone in this Arctic environment. His visit had quite an effect on me. For some reason after this encounter my own mild sense of isolation was greatly eased.

I was beginning to see that having purpose and appreciation seemed to be a source of strength for him enduring what appeared on the surface to be hardship. I am sure he did not view his routine as being onerous. He seemed to be truly at ease with this environment and was likely enjoying every moment of his work. No doubt he was motivated by other personal goals, but he did not share them with us.

I began to see this Arctic milieu in a slightly different way. I was beginning to understand and appreciate my own stay at Hadley Bay as remarkable. An opportunity had been presented to me with this job with Spartan. My new awareness had finally begun to sink in a little bit to reveal a much bigger picture about life and living.

Chapter 9

The Rings

We discovered a stone cairn just north of our weather station on a point of land. Was it a storage container of some kind? Its purpose was not obvious. The first thing we did was to look inside. This artefact stood a little over four and a half feet high, enclosed a smallish empty volume, and had a large flat shale stone for a lid. Smaller dinner-plate size pieces of shale used in the construction of its sides were covered with lichens indicating it had been there for some time. This marker stood like a lone sentinel looking out over the estuary and the Arctic Ocean beyond. Perhaps it was some sort of signpost for travellers, but its function was hidden from us. Was it indicating the direction to the Northwest Passage further north at the mouth of Hadley Bay? The existence of this weathered monument indicated this location had been visited much earlier. We were not the first as we have previously thought.

Our location at Hadley Bay was truly remote being just west of the north magnetic pole and many miles north of Cambridge Bay. Apparently, the magnetic north pole is in constant motion, moving several miles over the course of a decade or so. Our weather station was at the southern end of the Bay near the mouth of a river. We had named this river the Hadley River. Further to the north was the location of the famous Northwest Passage channel the search of which by the Franklin Expedition occurred over a hundred and fifty years ago. The old newspaper accounts of this fateful expedition had been spellbinding for many aspiring adventurers throughout the world.

The Franklin Expedition's purpose had been to find a route through Canada's ice-bound Arctic Islands by traversing a Northwest Passage from the Atlantic Ocean to the Pacific Ocean. Franklin's attempt had failed. All the people of this expedition were lost and their fate unknown at the time and for many years afterwards. The exact circumstances and details of this historic expedition's failure and loss of lives still remains a mystery.

Franklin's expedition was a British voyage of Arctic exploration led by Captain Sir John Franklin that departed England in 1845 aboard two ships, HMS Erebus and HMS Terror. A royal Navy officer and experienced explorer, Franklin had meant to discover and navigate a passageway through the icebound islands of the Canadian Arctic. After some severe weather difficulties in the ice-clogged channels the two ships became ice-bound in Victoria Strait somewhere near King William Island. The entire expeditionary force comprising 129 men including Franklin was lost.

The onset of our Arctic spring had brought on some warmer weather with daytime temperatures hovering around the freezing point. The spring run-off was occurring. The myriad of shallow sloughs and ponds around our weather station were gradually losing their ice-cover and becoming occupied with nesting birds, ducks, and geese aplenty. The terrain around Hadley Bay seemed to be very active with wildlife of all sorts which could have provided food for Inuit hunting groups if they could get there through the ice clogged bays or overland across many miles of rough terrain. This abundance could also have provided sustenance for Franklin's marooned sailors years ago. We saw seals out on the ice of the bay, ducks and geese everywhere, as well as ptarmigans, sea birds, Arctic hares and foxes, lemmings, and, of course, the occasional solitary transiting polar bear. Life with its predators was stirring all around us.

In spite of the threat posed by the polar bears I felt it was time to trek around the southern shoreline to the mouth of our so-called Hadley River a little more than a mile or so to the south of our weather station. We could take a look and maybe try some fishing. Marley and I had been essentially prisoners at our camp out of fear of the bears. In any case the plan would include taking the 30-30 with us while keeping a sharp lookout while exploring at the river mouth. We could hike over and have a look at the region and return to make our next weather report with time to spare. But Marley refused to go. "Not interested," was all he said. I was on my own.

The hike around to the mouth of the Hadley River took me longer than I had thought but I soon approached the rushing water of the river which over time had gouged a channel through the limestone and plate-like shale. The rock-scattered landscape offered little opportunity for tundra or moss-like growth on the riverbank. But there were fish. I believe they were Arctic Char on their way up the river to spawn. Soon, after a few casts, two fish was my reward, my only thought being could I carry this unwieldy load back to camp without too much difficulty. The fish looked appetizing and would provide us with some fresh food for a change.

Here, on the riverbank of our Hadley River was an expanse of flat bare limestone with the water gushing downstream several feet below the riverbank's level. It was at this point I noticed the circles or rings of rocks. Along the riverbank on top of a flat limestone area were two distinct circular rock formations consisting of many flat stones configured in two separated circles each about eight feet or so across. I was startled by the pattern. It was obvious they had been placed this way by someone. Their location and geometric regularity suggested some sort of purpose behind their formation.

I speculated these rocks may have been used to hold down the canvass or material of tents, or animal skin dwellings to secure the structures against the wind and weather. Then again for that matter I had no knowledge of Inuit dwellings or the tents of mid-nineteen century stranded expeditionary sailors. The circular rings of rocks exhibited some sort of unknown function and definitely had been placed there by someone.

My concern to get back to camp to make the next radio schedule led me to disregard a more careful study of these rings. As I trudged back with the fish for our next meal, I was puzzled by what I had seen on the riverbank. The circumstances underlying these circles or rings of rocks remains a mystery with me to this day.

Chapter 10

"Bushed"

I think I was beginning to feel the effects of being separated from my family and friends. I really was looking forward to getting back home. "One hundred fucking days! Seems like a helluva lot more," grumbled Marley.

My reply, "I haven't been counting, but that seems about right." I knew Marley was more upset than me.

Our weather station had been operating steadily since early-June but now it was much later, a week or so into August with the indications of winter coming on. In taking the job I had not really thought much about the effects of prolonged separation from my loved ones. My purpose was financing myself and gaining work experience with this summer job. I had not considered the adverse effects of being removed from my way of living. I did not think very much about the effect these deprivations would have on me or the possibility of me becoming "bushed". The term "*bushed*" can be inadequately defined as an adverse psychological condition brought on by the absence of a normal way of living due to prolonged isolation.

"We've finished off the Crispy Crunch©," declared Marley. For me, this unusual statement was completely unexpected and followed just after his "One hundred fucking days!" declaration. I wondered what he really meant by the "Crispy Crunch©" reference. Later, out of curiosity I checked our provisions and found the empty chocolate bar box confirming his comment. At the beginning of our stay at Hadley, the box had contained twelve Crispy Crunch© chocolate bars, and I was looking forward to eating my share. I reckoned I would like to try spreading the eating of my six bars over the duration of our stay. But Marley had consumed his share and my remaining bars as well. This selfishness made me angry. "Anger because of chocolate bars," was a telling reaction.

I had not though that much about being isolated. In fact, the solitude gave me time to prepare for a very challenging course in Matrices and Linear Transformations in my mathematics' studies for next year. I had brought the textbook along to prepare. I found our radio and weather work was quite routine and I could handle it easily with practically no difficulty. But Marley must have struggled. I did not really notice his difficulties, not that I could have done much about the situation.

Marley unexpectedly declared, "I think I could walk out to Cambridge. Its only about two hundred miles. But the terrain is rough with a lot of lakes to walk around. Maybe two weeks at most." Over the course of time, he had raised this possibility more than once.

I thought, "How whacky is this?" In my view walking out would be almost impossible.

The powerful single-engine Otter equipped with skis with its great manoeuvrability had brought us to Hadley.

We landed bumping and swerving over the pressure ridges of heaved ice. Ken Bolem was a skilful pilot. He could land and take-off from practically any place. He revved the engine and taxied across to what appeared to be the slightly elevated hump of land. This location would have to suffice. It would be our tiny isthmus where we would set up the weather station and spend quite some time doing our job.

The rocky terrain of the low peninsula was mainly obscured by ice and drifted snow. We had found it difficult to be absolutely certain all our supplies and camp gear were secure on dry land when we unloaded, specifically the two forty-five-gallon drums with the gasoline for the Onan generator and the fuel-oil for the tent stoves. Each weighed over 200 lbs. If we had guessed wrong these two heavy items would be difficult to move from the slippery ice onto dry land later as break-up occurred. This possible problem was an underlying worry. Marley would often dwell on this concern. I'm sure this situation only contributed to his upset. As it turned out when the snow and ice eventually melted away, we had guessed right about the location for the unloaded heavy drums. All was secure on the isthmus with our weather station above the high-water tides of the Bay.

With the onset of the Arctic summer in late June some of the ice at the mouth of the river began to open up a little. Ken's initial planning had called for our withdrawal from the weather station by Beaver on floats not much later than early-September. But, by mid-August, the gap of open water at the mouth of the estuary appeared to be far too small for the Beaver's landing and take-off requirements. Again, Marley's awareness of this situation must have just added to his underlying trouble. Also, the melting and fractured sea-ice further out on the Bay would likely be too unsafe to accommodate the weight of the heavier Otter with skis. The Otter is about twice the size of the Beaver. This predicament was just another concern. Marley must have worried if we really had a way out before freeze-up. Waiting for the next season's freeze-up in October would be an unthinkable situation to endure.

"Let's get the hell out of here!" Marley uttered in his frustration as he finished his shift and was heading to the other tent to sleep. He was disturbed. I guess he was just trying to cope with the situation, but his acceptance of this reality was not going well.

The massive ice-slurry on the bay, the remnants of the ice covering the estuary near the likely take-off area for the Beaver on floats, drifted about depending on the wind direction and potentially could pose a real hazard for landing and take-off. This mass of ice would blow from one side of the scant open water of the bay to the other side depending on the tides and the wind's strength and direction. The open water would have to broaden considerably, or our departure would certainly be delayed. I'm sure the sum of all these concerns only added to Marley's distressed frame of mind.

Marley would often remark, "Goddammed weather." For days on end the cloud layer would descend to just several hundred feet and sometimes with fog. No sunshine. I'm certain these conditions only heightened Marley's anxiety. But I still thought he could manage. In talking with him over the course of time I discovered he had some other disturbing issues.

He was originally from Ireland where he had lived near the border separating the two Irelands, Northern Ireland, and the Republic of Ireland. I soon learned he hated the British. In our conversations he described their military presence as a ruthless occupying force suppressing and brutally controlling the people of his beloved homeland. I caught a glimpse of this intolerance when we both sat recording weather traffic from the radio network. The radio operator at Pelly Lake giving the weather summary had an English accent. "Fucking limey!" Marley suddenly erupted.

"What's the trouble?" My question opened the door for him to berate the British. He went on to tell me that one of his uncles had been severely beaten and imprisoned by the occupying British military years ago at the beginning of the "Troubles". He disclosed his whole family had run-ins with the British authorities and he detested the "fucking limeys". His reaction to this simple situation of a radio operator's English accent was extreme. His overt hatred was troubling.

It was about then I noticed more bazaar behaviour and I worried where it would eventually lead. Marley would sleep for long periods of time. We had divided the workload roughly in half with some variation depending on the situation. But Marley was sleeping his life away. When he was not working, he was sleeping. Somehow, I had to tread lightly and not make the situation worse, but I was aware there were limits to this approach. I guess I did not truly understand his predicament.

For me I openly expressed my feelings that I was finding our location at Hadley as a place revealing many interesting things. The stone cairn and the rings of rocks had provided evidence that the area once had been occupied, possibly by Inuit hunters or perhaps even by ice-bound Franklin's sailors. Marley would mildly disparage my interest in this "goddamned place and its artefacts."

I soon discovered Marley was preparing a radio message to our main base at Cambridge Bay for our next regular weather reporting transmission. "What's happening Marley?", I questioned.

He said, "Read this. What do you think?" He had composed a message in the form of a verse and was sending it to Cambridge. I read the message:

"Lack of oil for generator
Demands we close the fornicator."

I saw what Marley was really planning. He was desperately looking for a way out, and even lying about our situation was his tactic. I knew there was no oil problem but regarded his ruse as rather ingenious.

Ken Bolam and others at Cambridge would have some doubts about this situation and would begin to infer there was an underlying more serious problem brewing here at Hadley. I'm sure the deception would reveal a serious situation. It would show Marley's inner turmoil. Marley was definitely in trouble, and it was important to resolve the situation fast. Regardless there still remained the predicament of exactly how we would be withdrawn from the peninsula. Would Ken use the Otter on skis and land on the unsafe ice, or would he land the Beaver with floats in the scant open estuary? The gap of open water was insufficient for landing and take-off using the Beaver, and the ice pack likely was not solid enough to support the heavier weight of the Otter. What was the solution? There appeared to be no way out.

But Marley had another idea. Marley's plan was absolutely startling. He proposed, "Why not land the Otter using the skis with the regular wheels partially engaged on one of the ancient beaches?" His unusual idea made some sort of sense. The combination of the Otter's skis and the partial wheel engagement would help with a landing on a short landing strip. The wheels would partly dig in and the skis would limit deeper gouging. The Otter would just skid to a stop.

Even though there was a moderate ocean tide at Hadley Bay, the high tide's water-level did not rise anywhere near the location of these prehistoric grit and sandy beaches. These beaches were formed or deposited over a long course of time thousands of years ago. These rather numerous ancient parallel narrow strips of beaches, each comprised mainly of loose layers of fine sand and gravel, were apparently laid down by a combination of the receding polar glaciers and the sand and grit formed by the Arctic Ocean's normal tidal action.

As the polar glaciers had receded the planet's crust or landmass rose up with the diminishing weight of the glacier's ice and, over time, the beaches formed one after another over thousands of years with the tidal action. These beaches gradually formed and lifted upward until they were left high and dry well above the present sea-level of the Arctic Ocean.

Some of these beaches were hundreds of feet in length although fairly narrow, at most about fifty feet wide. Marley envisioned they would make an excellent landing strip for the versatile Otter on skis and an adept pilot like Ken Bolam. I watched Marley as he picked the largest beach for the proposed landing strip and paced it off.

"Eight- hundred feet or slightly more. Fairly smooth full length," he said, "with a little more of rougher beach here and there."

I had no idea about the landing and take-off specifications on fine grit and gravel for the powerful single-engine STOL (short take-off and landing) Otter on skis with the wheels partially engaged. Maybe Marley knew something about these conditions, maybe not. Soon he was on the radio to Cambridge with his scheme. I'm sure his outlandish plan however viable was also revealing his inner turmoil to those at Cambridge Bay. I wondered what he was going to do if his plan was rejected.

Later that day Ken Bolam came on the VHF radio to talk directly to me. Marley was asleep in the other tent.

"Is the beach eight hundred feet?"

I confirmed that it was. "It is fairly narrow in some places, about forty or fifty feet wide or so. It seems pretty solid."

"How does Marley seem?" he asked. I then knew that the people at Cambridge understood that Marley had a problem. He was "bushed." He was becoming seriously affected and unable to cope. People becoming "bushed" was not all that uncommon. Perhaps Ken Bolam had encountered this situation before.

"He is really upset. Distressed, desperate I think."

"We will be there tomorrow with the Otter if the weather holds, and I'll also have a look at that open water at the river mouth for the Beaver later. Hang in there." I felt relieved. It was reassuring the base camp knew about the real problem and were trying to fix it.

Chapter 11

The Ancient Beach

The next morning the Otter took off from Cambridge Bay and sometime later droned in from the south. It circled our location while Ken surveyed the landing and take-off conditions at the mouth of the river, and then next the landing suitability on the ancient beech. Was the expanse of open water now sufficient for the Beaver's landing and take-off for early September? Was the beach landing a definite possibility. No doubt Ken was carefully assessing the situation.

Marley was racing about waving his arms as Ken flew overhead.

"Tell him to stand at the end of the beach where I will touch down.", radioed Bolam on UHF. "And tell him to get the hell out of the way as I approach." I yelled these instructions to Marley.

The Otter came into the ancient beach with the touch of a feather hitting the landing perfectly. The Otter slipped and skidded along and somewhat shallowly dug into the fine sand and grit but landed successfully after having used up only a small portion of the ancient narrow beach. The plane did not stop. Ken revved the engine and taxied back to the touchdown spot and turned the plane around into the wind.

The plane stopped and three occupants got out, Ken Bolam, Mike Grey our Spartan boss, and Pete Spicer, a radio tech from Cambridge Bay. We finally had some company. We shook hands and stood around talking about the landing and the open water situation at the mouth of the river. They then presented a container of several fresh loaves of bread, some soft-drinks, and, of course, several cans of oil for the Onan.

The plan was that Marley would return to Cambridge in exchange for Pete Spicer who would remain at Hadley Bay with me for the next two weeks or so depending on the weather opportunities for photographing and the open water conditions on the estuary. There still could be some photo-sorties for the Mossies to complete weather permitting. After all was said and done, the unfinished photo-lines would have to wait for next season. The two weeks would also provide more time for the ice on the estuary to clear. Ken indicated Pete Spicer and I would likely be taken out by the Beaver on floats in about two weeks. He had already surveyed the open-water landing options in his flyby. The landing and take-off possibilities on the estuary for the Beaver were promising.

Marley was ready to leave. He seemed satisfied with the developments. For me, I envied him getting back to Cambridge Bay and going south. I still had at least two more weeks at Hadley Bay.

Chapter 12

Withdrawal

By mid-September Spartan's photo season in the high Arctic Islands had come to an end. The weather had worsened as the climate made its way toward winter with the low-level overcast cooler conditions and the inadequate sun-angles with the shortening daylight. These signs of the approaching winter were unmistakable. But the summer had yielded some good flying days and only a few photo-contracts remained, possibly for next year's work. Over the summer season our Hadley Bay weather reports for the Arctic Forecast Team in Edmonton had enabled accurate predictions of good photo-mapping opportunities throughout the vast Arctic region. Now it was time to leave. Besides the receding daylight, the winds were becoming more biting, and the temperatures were dipping below freezing. I was eager to get home, back to my family and friends.

Ken Bolam had thought the small expanse of ice-free water at the mouth of our Hadley River would get no larger and would have to suffice for his landing and take-off platform. The aircraft to get us out was to be the intrepid Beaver on floats. For the past day an east wind had blown the ice-pack slurry away from our shore making the Beaver's landing and loading right up at our rocky peninsula possible. This was good news. We had radioed this fortunate situation to Cambridge, and everyone welcomed the opportunity to get started with our removal right away.

Later next morning, the Beaver turned into the wind, came in low over the ice slurry on the estuary and prepared to land in the open stretch of water right up to our weather station. The Beaver with its huge floats touched down, skimmed, and then ploughed up near our shore. Ken cut the engine and climbed down onto the starboard float and threw me the line. "I sure hope the wind holds and keeps that ice off this shore otherwise we will be here 'til next summer." I guessed his wry sense of humour was an attempt at alleviating our concern.

Pete Spicer and I were ready to get our departure done. There were no more weather observations or radio transmissions to be made, no photo-missions to be flown by our Mosquitos, no more air-traffic control. Winter was definitely coming fast, and I was looking forward to getting back home after having spent about one-hundred and twenty days at Hadley Bay. I did not want to be delayed by the pack of ice shifting onshore and closing off the already limited gap of open water we still had available for take-off. According to Ken the laden Beaver would require the largest expanse of open water available to get us airborne. We wasted no time loading and balancing the aircraft with only a limited portion of our total camp equipment.

Apparently, the Beaver is almost overloaded with just its floats alone. As a result, we were going to leave most of the bulky heavy equipment behind at our deserted weather station. The Beaver, much smaller than the Otter, could not accommodate the tents and frames, stoves, the heavy Onan power generator, and any other hulking gear we had brought in on several trips by the Otter in mid-May. The Beaver has about half the cargo capacity as the Otter. The take-off manoeuvring would require a much lighter aircraft with the limited open water we had available.

We loaded the radio transceivers and power supplies, the weather equipment, and our personal belongings. The station would be used next season, so we had carefully stowed the equipment we were leaving behind to secure it against the advancing winter. In less than an hour we were loaded up and we climbed into the aircraft.

The floats seemed to run the full length of the Beaver and made it seem unwieldy. I was last in after pushing us off from the rocky shore and paddling the aircraft around in the direction of the open water. Ken started the engine and taxied us out into the gap. We moved out to the edge of the slurry, turned back into the wind. Our take-off would be right over our vacated weather station. According to Ken, the take-off airspeed of the Beaver can be as low as about sixty knots depending on the wind. We would need all the room available. "Let's get 'er done," uttered Ken as he engaged the Beaver's throttle.

Slowly the aircraft ploughed forward. It seemed to wallow in the water like a great noisy walrus as the airspeed indicator slowly crept upward. The campsite was quickly approaching. At this point Ken backed-off the throttle and said we needed to lighten the load. Something had to go, like, the radio gear with its heavy power supplies and the weather equipment. In total the equipment we unloaded weighed over one-hundred and fifty pounds, about the weight of a person. We carefully stowed this discarded gear next to the power generator at the vacated weather station.

Again, we boarded, taxied across the gap, and turned back into the wind. This time just as we turned Ken noticed that one of the front wheel casters on the starboard float was turned awkwardly. This particular Beaver aircraft was equipped to land in water with floats, like, at our Hadley Bay location, or at Cambridge Bay on the DEW-line site's gravel runway with its two main wheels engaged plus the two front wheel casters when the aircraft was taxiing. The two front wheel casters could be activated and were essential for a normal four-point gravel runway landing and taxiing. Over the noise of the engine Ken yelled at me "Tom, turn the caster."

I climbed out onto the float and cautiously crouched my way up just behind the turning propeller and grabbed onto the caster. It wouldn't budge. I struggled with it. The front wheel casters were activated by some sort of hydraulic mechanism which could be engaged by the pilot just before landing. The two main wheels touched down first then forward onto four wheels on the runway. After seeing my struggles Ken signalled me back inside. "Leave it," he yelled. "It will probably work when we land." The word "probably" left some disquieting doubt in my mind.

Once back inside and buckled in Ken revved the engine and again, we ploughed forward into the wind, the engine roaring. This time Ken attempted to rock the Beaver from side to side from one float to the other in hopes of eventually getting the airplane up onto one float thereby reducing the drag considerably. If the tactic worked in time, we would achieve take-off.

The campsite rushed to meet us once again as the airspeed indicator crept upward. Finally, skimming on one float we slowly lifted off, lumbering into the air. We were flying. As the campsite swept by under us, I heard a noise.

Ken settled the mystery immediately. "There goes the UHF radio antenna, but we seem to be okay." Apparently one of the floats had clipped off the vertical radio mast at our abandoned weather station. We turned south. Soon we would be back at Cambridge Bay and on our way out. The uncooperative right-front wheel caster was my only concern now, but it was already too late to do anything about it.

Chapter 13

Ken Bolam

Back in the pre-satellite era, Spartan Air Service made its money providing precise high-altitude photographs including photographic images of the Arctic Archipelago. I was under the impression some of this aerial photography had been first carried out by the RCAF's 408 squadron earlier and the task was later taken over by Spartan Air Services. The Canadian government's mapping agency used this photographic information to make its topographical maps. Map detail was important. At the time Canadian sovereignty, mainly our shared international Arctic border with the US and USSR as well as Cold War issues, were the underlying political reasons for this costly operation.

The exacting photography necessary for making topographical maps required the efficient application of accurate weather forecasting. Predicting acceptable mapping weather conditions over a Northern and high Arctic region had an enormous bearing on profitability. The Canadian Arctic region encompasses about 40% of Canada's total land mass. It is a vast area. This immense remote region at this point in time had very few regular DOT (Department of Transport) weather stations from which to get comprehensive and contiguous weather data for forecasting. Spartan had planned to set up two temporary weather stations to fill in these weather reporting gaps.

This additional weather information was to be gathered by these temporary stations and sent to the Arctic Forecast Team in Edmonton to be integrated with their other DOT information. Forecasting was important because precise high-altitude photography required clear cloudless weather, a minimum of ice and snow ground coverage, very little smoke interference from forest fires (a definite problem below the treeline) and optimum sun angles (no shadows allowed) for Spartan's Mosquito aircraft to do the job.

Spartan Air Services had subcontracted Ken Bolam, a Pacific Western Airways' pilot and project manager, to supervise the installation of the two proposed temporary weather stations. One weather station was to be located at Hadley Bay on the northern shore of Victoria Island and the other at Fisher Lake on Prince of Wales Island just west of Sommerset Island. Spartan's high-altitude Mosquito aircraft would fly their photo-line sorties from the southern centrally located Distant Early Warning or DEW-line site airfield located at Cambridge Bay on the south coast of Victoria Island.

I was hired as one part of a two-person team to install and operate one of these weather stations at some suitable location (the exact location to be determined by actual observation when we got to an appropriate site) somewhere on the north shore of Victoria Island. Victoria Island is Canada's second largest island, it being about twice the size of Nova Scotia. The approximate location for the proposed weather station was little over two hundred nautical miles north of Cambridge Bay at about 71°N latitude and 107°W longitude near our planet's north magnetic pole.

I flew via TCA, Trans Canada Airlines as it was called back in the day from Ottawa to Edmonton and then PWA, Pacific Western Airlines, to Yellowknife and on to Cambridge Bay. Cambridge Bay, a DEW-line site, is situated on Victoria Island across the Coronation Gulf from Canada's mainland. It was at Cambridge Bay where I first met Spartan's project manager Ken Bolam, and the other person of our two-person weather team, Gene Marley.

Ken Bolam was a PWA "bush" pilot even though his many flying, management, and leadership skills were brought to bear well above the Arctic Circle where the nearest bush or tree was a thousand miles to the south. As Spartan's project manager, Ken's task was seeing to the installation of the two temporary weather stations. He piloted both the Otter and Beaver service aircraft for these installations, his job being to assemble the weather station equipment at Cambridge and ferry it and its personnel, Marley and me, to a suitable site at Hadley Bay. The other temporary weather station was to be set up at Fisher Lake further to the east on Prince of Wales Island. It was mid-May and hopefully these two installations would be done and dusted by the end of the month. Also, he would direct the task of removing these weather stations and personnel before freeze-up in late-September.

A few years later while drinking some draughts at The Manor, a Kingston pub, with some of my former Spartan buddies at a reunion of sorts, I learned that Ken Bolam had been killed. Apparently, Ken had been run down by a car while crossing the street near his home in Vancouver. This terrible news was absolutely shocking. Somehow it did not seem believable he had exited from life in this way. Those of us around the table thought his untimely death should have somehow been related to his flying. Flying can be risky but sometimes risks must be taken. Ken had been a moderate risk taker when we worked with him. Those of us who knew him recognized his zest for living and appreciated him as an exceptional leader and gifted flyer. But most of all he was a good human being, a smart honest hard worker, a leader you could count on. In thinking about this sad situation, we began to reminisce around the table about those times working with Ken at Cambridge Bay and further north. We began to tell our stories.

When it came time to tell my story I recalled for the group the time Ken was getting our weather station set up on the north shore of Victoria Island. In my imagination, it was mid-May once again years ago. We were ferrying our weather station equipment via the Otter on skis. There was plenty of winter remaining with snow and ice still covering Hadley Bay, our non-specific landing destination where we would set up our weather station. The Otter, piloted by Ken, was a high-wing, propeller-driven, short take-off and landing (STOL) aircraft. Normally it would seat about ten passengers but with the seats removed it was an exceptional cargo aircraft with great capability, a real workhorse flying machine for transporting our weather station's equipment. I recalled for the group the myriad of planning details as I recounted my story.

Ken said, "It will take several flights." Ken and Mike Gray, Ken's supervisor from Spartan, were planning our insertion to Hadley Bay from our main base at Cambridge Bay using the Otter on skis, the distance being a little over two-hundred nautical miles to the north. "The first load should carry the gasoline and fuel oil drums, the stoves, and the bulky tents as well as Tom and Marley. With the second load we can take the Onan generator with the transceivers, the VHF and UHF transceivers, antennas, and weather equipment...."

I remember Ken turning to us. "You two will unload the gear and start the set up. The first thing to do is to put up the tents so you can get out of the weather if it turns ugly while I'm getting the next load. Keep in mind we've got to finish by early June at the latest."

Marley and I were to setup and operate this Hadley Bay weather station. After the setup our job was to collect daily weather information and report it to our main base in Cambridge Bay by VHF radio. The weather reports from Hadley, and Fisher Lake, that other temporary weather station several hundred miles to the east, would then be sent to the Arctic Forecast Team in Edmonton for their analysis. Giving these routine weather reports would be our job for the next three months. We were to load up the powerful Otter at Cambridge Bay, a DEW-line site with a gravel runway, fly to Hadley Bay, look for a suitable location and land on the ice close to the chosen site, unload the aircraft, and begin the setup while the Otter returned to Cambridge for the next load. Weather permitting, this process was to be repeated over the better part of two weeks or so until the weather station was installed and reporting.

I recalled for my group of patient listeners that Ken had been flying steadily with the installation of the other weather station at Fisher Lake located on Prince of Wales Island further to the east across the McClintock Channel. Now he was setting up our station at Hadley Bay. The twenty-four hours of daylight at this mid-May time of year made the working part of the day seem much longer. He had been flying steadily for days. Ken looked tired. We all realized the necessity of getting things finished as quickly as possible because you never knew when the weather was going to worsen and delay these installations even more.

To navigate the approximately two-hundred nautical miles from Cambridge Bay to Hadley Bay Ken was using the Otter's sextant to estimate the aircraft's position. A sextant is a compact sun-sighting mechanism used for measuring the angular distances between objects on the planet to determine latitude and longitude. The sextant was mounted on the left side of the inner windscreen of the Otter. He would take sun-shots every so often to estimate the location of the aircraft. The intended site for our weather station was somewhere near the south end of Hadley Bay but, of course, its exact location would be established only after we had scoped out a suitable site. The Bay ran south to north eventually opening up to the Arctic Ocean just south of Melville Island to the north and was a relatively large, elongated body of water and would be fairly easy to locate because of its size.

The maps Ken was using, originally photographed by the RCAF's 408 Squadron a few years before, were incomplete. They provided just imprecise outlines of the Arctic terrain. In fact, Spartan Air Services was in the process of getting the raw photographs to be used in making accurate topographical maps of this vast Arctic region. At this point in time, we were unaware these mapping methods Spartan was presently using would soon become obsolete with the application of the new emerging satellite technology. My story about Ken continued as my buddies offered the occasional one-liner or wisecrack about my descriptions. I continued to describe to the group the problems of Ken's navigation to Hadley Bay.

The magnetic compass in the Otter was useless because of our proximity to the north magnetic pole. Of course, the Earth's north magnetic pole is always in a constant state of flux vis-à-vis location and magnetic strength variability. It apparently moves miles in the course of a decade or so. In any event the Otter's compass wandered all over the place and offered no reliable information for helping Ken's navigation. Navigating was reduced to Ken using a combination of the sun-shots with the sextant and the wind and air speed directions for some kind of approximate positioning.

As we flew north, I remembered that the weather was closing in. It was necessary for Ken to manoeuvrer the Otter around to find an opening where he could get a decent sun-shot. Once the sun was in view he would make his sextant readings, confirm our location, and continue on toward our destination. Weather permitting, finding Hadley Bay did not require pinpoint accuracy. Our proposed destination was to be somewhere near the southern end of the Bay near a river estuary. The sextant's accuracy would easily get us to this location. Then we would search the area for a good site for the weather station. As we flew northward, I noticed Ken leaning at the port window taking the sextant's reading. I guessed he was still having difficulty in finding openings to view the sun because of the thickening clouds. Ken had to shout over the Otter's engine roar, "If it gets any worse, we'll have to turn back."

A little later I sensed the aircraft easing left. I looked over at Ken and saw him leaning near the port window presumably taking sextant readings. I knew he was having difficulty searching for an opening but soon the plane was drifting to the left abnormally. I looked more closely at him and discovered he was asleep. I reached over and shook him, and he wakened with a start. He must have been asleep for some time. Immediately he began searching for the sun. He increased the altitude a little but no luck. The thick dark clouds were completely blocking the sun. "I'm not sure where we are. Let's go down and have a look."

In winter the central and western Arctic terrain of Victoria Island is featureless. It is relatively flat with no mountains and the outlines of iced-over rivers and lakes are difficult to see. In the Arctic summer there are thousands of sloughs or tiny lakes but in mid-May they are still covered over. We were confronted with featureless white-grey terrain in all directions. Which way to go?

Ken turned the Otter and flew in a direction presumably back on course. In about an hour I saw the coastline appear and Ken brightened. "Okay, we are home free now." He turned at the coastline and within ten minutes or so, much to my astonishment, I saw the DEW-line site at Cambridge Bay with its gravel runway reappear. I was dumbfounded because we had taken off from this location about an hour before. I had thought we were still headed to Hadley Bay on the north coast of the island two-hundred miles away in the opposite direction. No doubt we would try again when the weather improved. The details of my story had been interspersed with some light-hearted sporadic quips from my listeners. These banters are the way of compatriots. This first unsuccessful flight to Hadley Bay mainly recognized Ken's determination, courage, risk taking, and flying expertise.

Then several in the group had a few more stories of their own to tell as the carousing and conversation continued. As the evening progressed, we had all joined in to tell our tales, to recall those times, to inject some degree of humour in our attempt to assuage our feelings of the loss of a friend. In a way these stories had taken on a genuine light-hearted honest tribute to Ken Bolam.

As his compatriots we were like a clan or family gathered at their campfire back in those ancient times, telling stories, harkening back to significant happenings. Were we just recalling the interesting and exciting times? We had gathered, staring into the embers of our younger lives with our steadily approaching middle-age perspective, searching our memories. Our stories were filled with humour and good will centred on Ken Bolam's influences. No doubt the reminiscing was embellished by the camaraderie and, of course, what was on tap. The many recollections of Ken Bolam's contributions came flooding back in the form of an appreciation of the brief but important example he had demonstrated. This harkening was now being stirred by the stark reality that he was no longer alive. Somehow his death seemed unsettling and unsettled. But now, here at the table in The Manor, we were saluting him. He still seemed to be with us.

Chapter 14

Retrospective

After flying south from Hadley Bay to Cambridge Bay to Yellowknife to Edmonton, and then eastward across Canada to Ottawa, I finally returned to Kingston and my home. During this return journey, I remember I had plenty of time to think about what I had experienced over the past two summer seasons working for Spartan in Canada's North. My take was, although some of the experiences had been challenging, I had greatly underappreciated them. Looking back and reconsidering what I had seen and done, I have since had many enjoyable rewarding recollections of the places, events, people, and memories to cherish. I now wish I had valued these experiences more while they were actually taking place.

Acknowledgements

I would like to thank the Writer's Rendezvous Group, my publisher and mentor Dorothyanne Brown, and my wife Janet, for the help they have given me in the writing and production of *The Spartan Chronicles*.

About the Author

Author Thomas Frood, while studying at Queen's University (physics and mathematics), began his job experiences working two seasons for Spartan Air Services as a weather observer and radio operator in Canada's north. His professional career was in mathematics education and as Head of a Mathematics Department. Throughout this career he spent much time contributing as a basketball coach. Hobbies include canoeing, banjo playing, and writing. He is retired and lives on a small farm near Wilton Ontario.

You can contact the author through the Somewhat Grumpy Press web site, www.SomewhatGrumpyPress.com.

Help independent authors and small presses by leaving reviews at your favourite retailers.

Milton Keynes UK
Ingram Content Group UK Ltd.
UKHW020245221123
432980UK00016B/976